# 50 ANIMAL PATTERNS
## Adult Coloring Book

An Adult Coloring Book Featuring 50 Fun and Relaxing
Animal Designs Including Horses, Bears, Tigers, Birds,
and Many More!

an Imprint of **The Fruitful Mind Publishing LTD.**
**www.coloringbookcafe.com**

Have questions? Let us know.
**support@coloringbookcafe.com**

 facebook.com/coloringbookcafe   @coloringbookcafe

This Book
Belongs To:

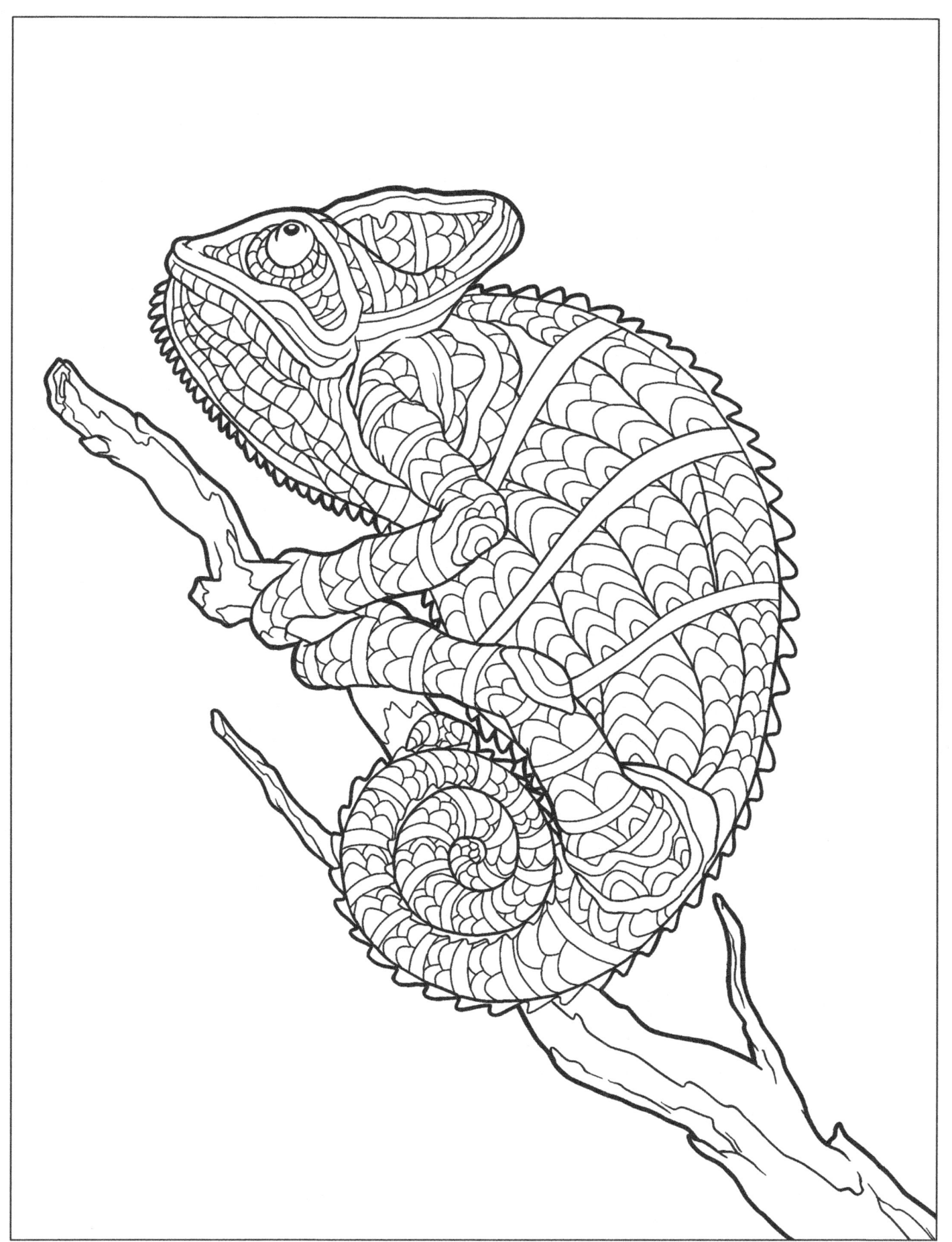

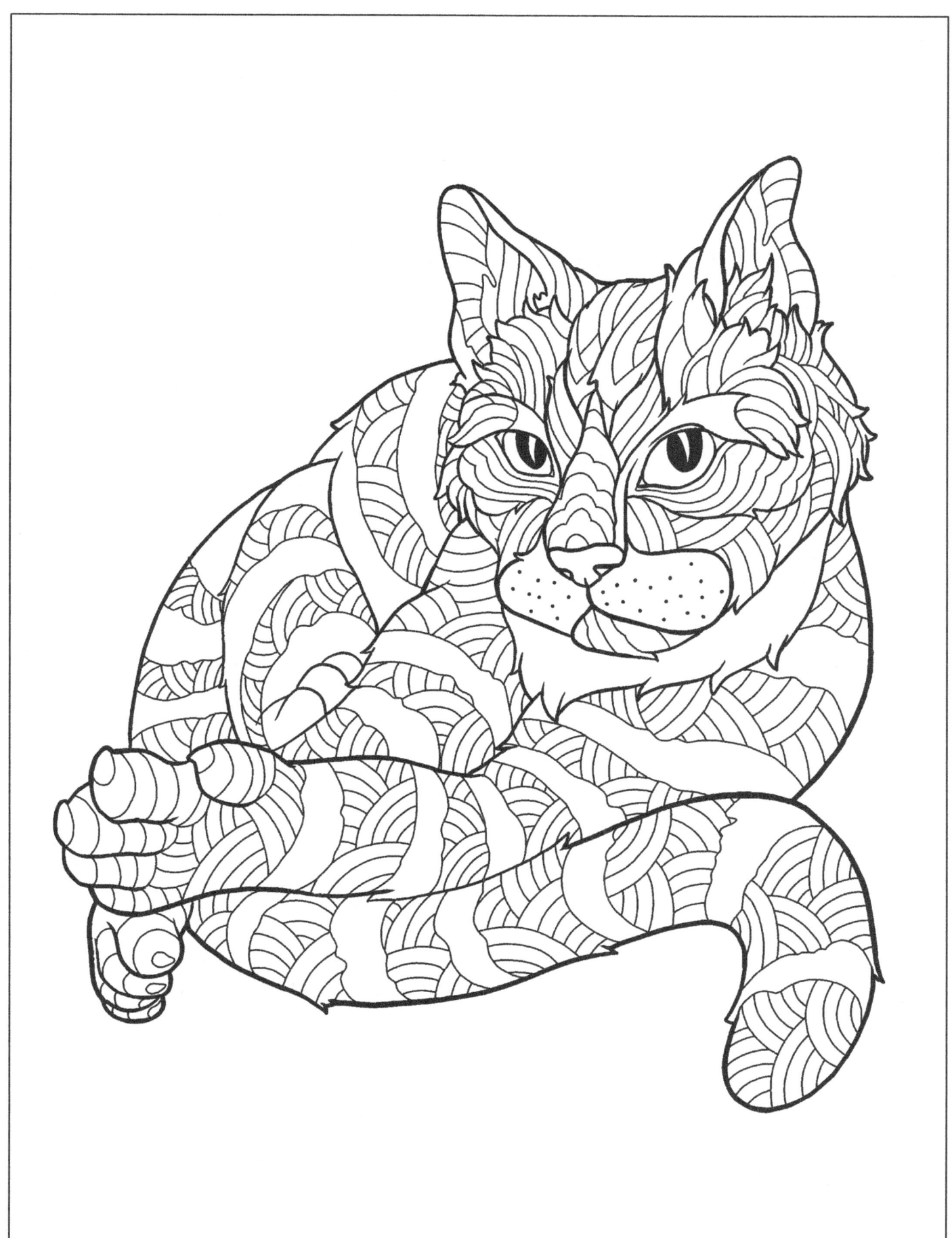

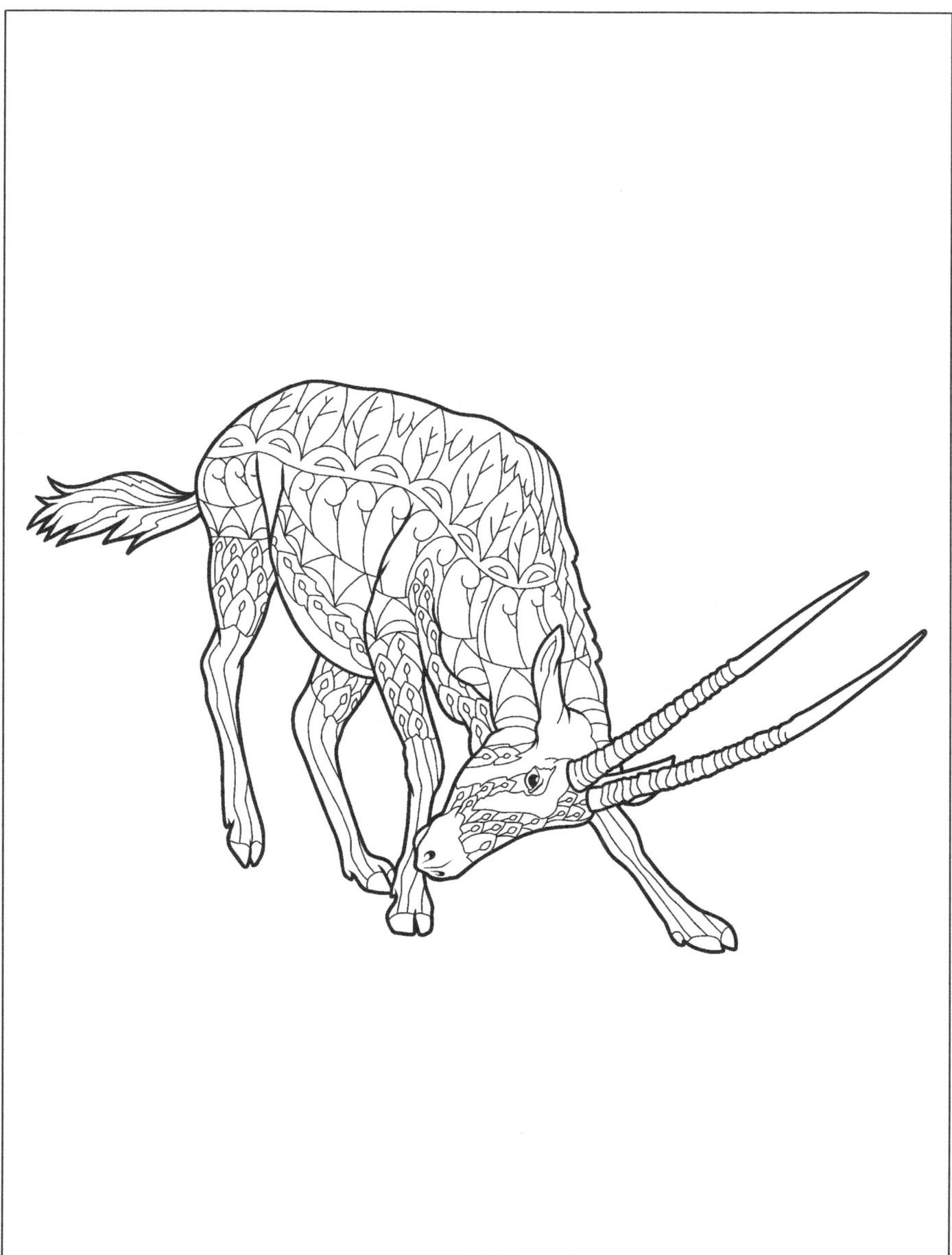

# COLOR CHART

Made in the USA
Monee, IL
22 January 2021